WHEN GOD DRAWS NEAR

REFLECTIONS ON THE INCARNATION

BY MARK HART

Unless otherwise noted, Scripture passages have been taken from the Catholic Edition of the Revised Standard Version of the Bible, copyright 1965, 1966 by the Division of Christian Education of the National Council of the Churches of Christ in the United States of America. Used by permission. All rights reserved.

Quotes are taken from the English translation of the Catechism of the Catholic Church for the United States of America (indicated as CCC), 2nd ed. Copyright ©1997 by United States Catholic Conference – Libreria Editrice Vaticana.

©2022 Life Teen, Inc. All rights reserved. No part of this book, including interior design, cover design, and/or icons, may be reproduced or transmitted in any form, by any means (electronic, photocopying, recording, or otherwise) without prior written permission from the publisher.

The information contained herein is published and produced by Life Teen, Inc. The resources and practices are in full accordance with the Roman Catholic Church. The Life Teen® name and associated logos are trademarks registered with the United States Patent and Trademark Office. Use of the Life Teen® trademarks without prior permission is forbidden. Permission may be requested by contacting Life Teen, Inc. at 480-820-7001.

Authored by Mark Hart

Cover Design & Interior Design: Scott Kerecman

Copy Edit: Rachel Peñate

Published by Life Teen, Inc. 2222 S. Dobson Rd. Suite 601 Mesa, AZ 85202 LifeTeen.com

Printed in the United States of America. Printed on acid-free paper.

TABLE OF CONTENTS

INTRODUCTION	6
HOW TO USE THIS RESOURCE	14
DAY ONE	16
DAY TWO	19
DAY THREE	23
DAY FOUR	27
DAY FIVE	31
DAY SIX	34
DAY SEVEN	38
DAY EIGHT	41
DAY NINE	44
DAY TEN	47

DAY ELEVEN	50
DAY TWELVE	53
DAY THIRTEEN	56
DAY FOURTEEN	59
DAY FIFTEEN	62
DAY SIXTEEN	66
DAY SEVENTEEN	69
DAY EIGHTEEN	72
DAY NINETEEN	75
DAY TWENTY	78
DAY TWENTY-ONE	81
DAY TWENTY-TWO	84
DAY TWENTY-THREE	87
DAY TWENTY-FOUR	90
DAY TWENTY-FIVE	94

INTRODUCTION

Why would God become a man? I mean, it's crazy when you think about it. The God of the universe coming to Earth in human form? Not on a cloud as a mighty conqueror, but as a fragile, dependent baby?!? Why would He make Himself so vulnerable? Why would the limitless, all-powerful Master of All — Creator of Creation — empty Himself like that?

Well, the answer begins with the Old Testament. Throughout those very first books of the Bible, we see clear examples of God reaching out to His people for their attention. He gives them paradise, but they screw it up. He blesses them, but they turn their backs. He frees them, but they turn their hearts. He feeds them, but they complain about the menu. He protects them, but they protect their own interests. He teaches them, but they close their ears. He warns them, but they tell Him they know better.

He treats them like children, but the kids turn into brats.

No matter how much God tried to rescue His chosen people, they found ways — created ways — to screw up the plan. So, why the Incarnation? Why did heaven take flesh and come to Earth?

Sacred Scripture unfolds the story for us perfectly. The saints add and share invaluable wisdom on the subject. Your own priest or other teachers of faith in your life have most likely weighed in on the topic, too, but somehow this all-important point is often lost: most Christmas hymns and carols tell of the "who" or the "what" that happened at Christmastime, but few actually get to the "why"?

Why did God take flesh? *Why did God draw near?*

Many years ago, I was listening to the radio as I drove back to work from lunch. It was an ordinary day in December — filled parking lots, overflowing shopping carts, and every person less patient than the one before him. The true spirit of Christmas was nowhere to be found, and my soul and heart were heavy (not to mention, stressed). It seemed as though the stress of gift-giving was flowing forth from a manger of materialism.

God Found a Way to Draw Near

It was at that moment that I switched the station to a famous broadcaster named Paul Harvey, and he shared a story that I will always remember:

"The man I'm going to tell you about was not a scrooge, he was a kind, decent, mostly good man. Generous to his family and upright in his dealings with other men. But he just didn't believe in all of that Incarnation stuff that the churches proclaim at Christmas time. It just didn't make sense and he was too honest to pretend otherwise. He just couldn't swallow the Jesus story, about God coming to Earth as a man.

He told his wife, 'I'm truly sorry to distress you, but I'm not going with you to church this Christmas Eve.' He said he would feel like a hypocrite and that he would much rather just stay at home, but that he would wait up for them. So he stayed and they went to the midnight service.

Shortly after the family drove away in the car,

snow began to fall. He went to the window to watch the flurries getting heavier and heavier and then he went back to his fireside chair and began to read his newspaper.

Minutes later, he was startled by a thudding sound. Then another ... and then another. At first he thought someone must be throwing snowballs against the living room window. But when he went to the front door to investigate he found a flock of birds huddled outside miserably in the snow. They'd been caught in the storm and in a desperate search for shelter they had tried to fly through his large landscape window. That is what had been making the sound.

Well, he couldn't let the poor creatures just lie there and freeze, so he remembered the barn where his children stabled their pony. That would provide a warm shelter. All he would have to do is to direct the birds into the shelter.

Quickly, he put on a coat and galoshes and he tramped through the deepening snow to the barn. He opened the doors wide and turned on a light so the birds would know the way in. But the birds did not come in.

So, he figured that food would entice them. He hurried back to the house and fetched some bread crumbs. He sprinkled them on the snow, making a trail of breadcrumbs to the yellow-lighted wide open doorway of the stable. But to his dismay, the birds ignored the bread crumbs.

The birds continued to flap around helplessly in the snow. He tried catching them but could not. He tried shooing them into the barn by walking around and waving his arms. Instead, they scattered in every direction ... every direction except into the warm lighted barn.

And that's when he realized they were afraid of him. To them, he reasoned, I am a strange and terrifying creature. If only I could think of some way to let them know that they can trust me. That I am not trying to hurt them, but to help them. But how? Any move he made tended to frighten them and confuse them. They just would not follow. They would not be led or shooed because they feared him.

He thought to himself, if only I could be a bird and mingle with them and speak their language. Then I could tell them not to be afraid. Then I could show them the way to the safe warm barn. But I would have to be one of them so they could see ... and hear ... and understand. At that moment the church bells began to ring. The sound reached his ears above the sounds of the wind. He stood there listening to the bells pealing Adeste Fidelis — the glad tidings of Christmas.

And he sank to his knees in the snow ..."

As I found out later, Paul, himself, did not author this narrative, and he spent years trying to find out who did — to no avail. The original author wanted to remain anonymous, merely desiring to share this story with the world.

While no analogy is perfect, this story does a great job in answering — with profound simplicity — this question of "why" Jesus took on our flesh in the Incarnation, and explaining the sacrificial love of God. When God took flesh and became like us in all things but sin (Hebrews 2:14-18) it revealed the lengths that God would go to in order to rescue us and the depths He would go to — even the very bowels of hell — to save us.

Our Salvation is His Desire

It's important to note, though, that God is still

on a rescue mission. God is still working harder for our salvation than we do, daily. He desires to save us from death, from sin, from pride ... He is trying to save us from our very selves and the season of Advent shines a light on this reality time and time again. We are called to contemplate not only what God did 2,000 years ago, but what He is still doing today!

So, stop, and ask yourself, "has God ever 'drawn near' to you?"

Many people talk often and easily about times they have encountered God — times they felt His presence or heard His voice. Countless books, movies, and songs have been written over the centuries attesting to the experiences people have had with God the Father, Jesus Christ His Son, and the Holy Spirit. These moments — if authentic and true — all had one thing in common: the person sharing about them had "eyes to see" or "ears to hear" (Matthew 13:15).

For us to see through the darkness of sin and evil and selfishness and pride, we need one thing ... light. More to the point, we need one person: the Light of the World, Jesus Christ.

He is Always Closer Than You Think

You might feel like God is very close to you right now; you might feel like God could not be more distant; or you might not be so sure about any of this. Wherever you are, currently, on your spiritual journey — however close you are to the Lord in your own mind and heart — know, that *He is near.* And, **He is always closer than you think, even on your best days.** As St. Catherine of Siena put it, "God is closer to us than water is to a fish." The challenge is to be so in tune with the Holy Spirit that we can actually see and hear Him, that we can perceive His movements and activity in our lives.

God is drawing near to you, again, this Advent season. Take a moment and ask the Holy Spirit to reveal to you all the ways God has and is drawing near. And with every turn of page in this book, rejoice that God not only took flesh but remains — in the flesh — in every Catholic tabernacle and altar across the globe ... for the manger is as close as your local parish.

If we are standing in the light, we can clearly see that God is still drawing near to His children.

HOW TO USE THIS COMPANION

This Advent companion is designed to be used daily, with 25 reflections in total. These are short reflections based on the mystery of the Incarnation and are written to give you a boost of inspiration at the start or end of your day.

Each reflection concludes with a small challenge that will help bring the reflection to life in your daily walk of faith.

Since this is a daily reflection, pick a time that you know you will remember to pray through the reflection of the day. If you are always rushing to get to school on time, trying to pray early in the morning probably isn't a good idea. If you are always exhausted right before you go to bed, waiting to pray at night probably won't work either. Be honest about when you can make the time (and focus).

Journey With Friends

We never journey alone. Find a small group of your friends or connect with peers from your youth group to pray through this Advent companion together. Discuss the reflections each week, remind one another to complete your challenge, and consider starting a group message to pray for each other and share encouragement. It is easy to feel isolated in our faith, but that is not how our faith is meant to be lived. Find other people to walk alongside you this Advent.

We are praying for you and walking with you, as well. Our team has put prayer and heart into this companion because we want to help you encounter Christ this Advent, just as we look forward to encountering Him, as well. Connect with us over social media to share how your journey is going @lifeteen and know that you are part of a bigger community and movement of young disciples that is connected across the world. It's time to take Advent seriously and joyfully — now go ahead and dive in!

DAY ONE

Think of the last time you were in a pitch black room. Really think back to a time and location with absolutely no light seeping in from any cracked open door or partly shaded window. No light emanating from an alarm clock display or phone screen on a table or nightstand. It's hard to imagine total darkness these days, given so many artificial sources of illumination that fill our lives and rooms, but picture yourself within that darkness, unsure which direction to head. Unable to move. Just alone, in the darkness, with no sense of direction and absolutely no light ... with no real hope or companionship ... just emptiness and loneliness and solitude. What a horrible place to be.

It was in this darkness that God first "drew near" and breathed the words, "Let there be light." When the Creator spoke, creation breathed. And, what followed was the unfolding of a perfect design from the divine designer — a design that began with intentionality and purpose and hope, a design that began with bringing light to the darkness.

That same creator and designer is a father who refuses to let His children persist in darkness. He desires that we are seen and He is known, so He breathed light into darkness with balls of fire we call stars, that we might not gaze upon the night sky and call it merely "space" but the heavens. He gave us light in the middle of our solar system not only to warm us but so that life could grow, for life without light is impossible. This father is so good and so loving that He even assigns us all our very own angel — carriers and ambassadors and guardians of light — so that we would not be lost or alone in seasons or moments of darkness.

This same designer placed a star high in the heavens not only to signal foreign missionaries where to find the Messiah, but for all to witness the good news. The star of Bethlehem became the most epic birth announcement in the history of humanity. In the Advent season, we see far more clearly and far more closely, the epic battle between darkness and light unfold. In Advent, we celebrate the Incarnation, as a sin-darkened world that waited countless centuries finally sees

God make good on His promise to send a Messiah and Savior.

Each day of the season of Advent, we allow in more light until the light shines forth for all to see on Christmas night.

MAKING IT PERSONAL

Where have you spent time in personal darkness? When has God's love or forgiveness breathed light into your life?

Stop and consider a time (or many times) and say a prayer thanking God for being a light in your darkness, or for sending someone — who is a light to you — to offer needed perspective at a specific time.

DAY TWO

Have you ever noticed, in the Book of Genesis, there are two distinct accounts of creation? Genesis chapter one and Genesis chapter two tell the same "story" of creation but with different details and from two very different vantage points. We may assume that either the writers of chapter two didn't "fact check" or verify sources for chapter one, or — perhaps — the author(s) are trying to teach us something significant.

The Old Testament basically uses two different words for God: Elohim and Yawheh. Now, to be clear, this is not meant to imply there are two Gods — not at all. There is one God and He does not have a multiple personality disorder. The two names are meant to reveal something to us about different characteristics about God: He is both creator and father.

In Genesis chapter one, the name used for God is Elohim. It refers to God's might and power as the creator of all creation. He is awesome and majestic and sovereign and powerful ... but seemingly "distant." He breathes the cosmos into existence and fashions stars and planets, land and sea, sky and animals and man. It's amazing and impressive, but in a way God seems almost inaccessible to us — like unapproachable light — unfathomable in might and unseeable by sight. Genesis chapter one shows us how grand God is but the connection ceases there. He is creator, and we are (immersed in His) creation.

When we turn the page to chapter two of Genesis, however, the writers switch gears and refer to God as Yahweh-Elohim. The designation Yahweh reveals even more about the Lord, as it is His personal name. Yahweh is used in the context of God having (and wanting) a relationship with His people. This is why — in chapter two — we see God "get His hands dirty." He doesn't just create from a distance, far from it (no pun intended). Yahweh puts His own hands into the dust of the Earth and breathes life into it, making Adam. Yahweh puts His hands into Adam's own side and removes a rib from within, fashioning Eve, the crown-jewel of creation and the most complex of all (for the woman would bear the unique and special distinction of being able to bring and bear life).

Between these two early chapters, we see God through two sides of the same coin. *He is both all-powerful and majestic but, also, accessible and magnificent.* The only warmth that outweighs the sun Elohim created is the warmth Yahweh's personal love offers. How can a God so large and powerful also be so loving and gentle?

In a few weeks, we will look to the manger and find our answer. The Incarnation — when God took flesh — is not only prophesied in Genesis chapter three when God promises to send us a Savior (3:15), but it's foreshadowed by God's own true self as seen by the names He reveals to us from the beginning.

MAKING IT PERSONAL

Looking at these two characteristics of God, which "vision of God" resonates more with you? The God who is mighty and distant and seemingly inaccessible? Or the God who has drawn near in the manger and tabernacle, who is approachable and accessible? Perhaps in your life it's even changed from one to the other at times. How do you think God wants you to view Him and come to Him, this day? Say a prayer and ask Him to show you.

DAY THREE

Do you ever feel like maybe God's just not "paying attention"? Like maybe, perhaps, God sort of tapped out, or isn't really watching, or just sort of hit the divine snooze button when it comes to your life? Have you ever looked up to the sky and wanted to shake your fist or just scream, "Hello?? Are you still there? Do you even care what's going on down here, Lord?"

Yeah, me, either (he said sarcastically).

It's easy to fall into the trap of thinking that God acts and reacts like we do. Nothing could be further from the truth. God is omniscient (all-knowing) and omnipotent (all-powerful). For "as the heavens are higher than the Earth, so are my ways higher than your ways and my thoughts higher than your thoughts" (Isaiah 55:9), says the Lord. God acts, yes, but He doesn't "react" the same way His creation does. God is always in control; He knows all and sees all. God's plan is perfect and His timing is flawless, we just don't understand it. Nothing surprises God. Nothing happens by coincidence. When we take a closer look at the story of Scripture, we see that even at the very beginning, when it seemed that the world was spinning out of control and Paradise was coming undone, God was very much in charge.

The Incarnation and the seasons of Advent and Christmas are about the fulfillment of God's plan and, more to the point, the fulfillment of His **promise** to us to send us a Savior. When sin entered the scene and Adam and Eve gave into pride, God did not abandon them. No, when sin ran rampant in the Garden of Eden and they allowed the darkness to overcome them, God showed up and revealed a plan to save them and, by extension, to save us.

Think about how amazing this news is for us. God doesn't turn His back on us even when we sin. There in Eden, as the darkness fell and the evidence of their disobedience was still apparent on their guilt-ridden faces, God promised to send a redeemer born of a woman (Genesis 3:15). Little did they know that not only did the Father have "an answer" but that He could become *the answer.* Even in their greatest moment of shame and hour of selfishness, God *drew near to them.*

This reality should bring us immense hope and consolation. You may believe that when you sinned, God gave up on you. You might mistakenly think that because of repeated sin God has abandoned all hope in you. You could not be more wrong. That's not who God is and it's definitely not how He thinks. Throughout the Bible, God keeps coming up with dramatic and miraculous ways to save His people from ruin, even though they're usually the very reason that the ruin came.

MAKING IT PERSONAL

Think of the worst thing you have ever done. If you have asked for forgiveness and gone to Confession, sincerely sorry for it, let it go. God has. If you have been too embarrassed to confess it, too ashamed, or haven't made time, make it a priority to get to the Sacrament right away, as soon as humanly possible. The Lord does not want you to be overwhelmed or anchored by this weight anymore. And if you have confessed it and Christ has already forgiven you through the ministry of the Church, but you've refused to forgive yourself, let it go once and for all. It's done. Ask Jesus for the grace you need to remove the boulder of guilt you're carrying and live in freedom. His plan is to save you, so let Him.

DAY FOUR

When you ask most people in the modern age about the existence of God (what He is "all about") or organized religion, one is often met with a certain degree of cynicism and negativity. Many reduce God merely to a divine judge condemning people to hell or some almost sadistic rule-giver who seeks only our misery. Sadly, the Church is often reduced, too, to a suspicious organization or cult whose only real goal is to control and abuse others into fear-filled submission.

Millions view God through the lens of "harsh judge in a courtroom," instead of a loving father in a living room. "Don't break the rules or God *(if there even is one)* will smite you!" seems to be the prevailing misunderstanding of the modern era. For these wounded and/or hardened souls who we usually see share their emptiness on our social media feeds, the idea of God drawing near would be utterly fictitious or, worse yet, horrifying.

When we don't like the idea of accountability that comes with letting God be God, it's easier to put God in a "box" of cruelty or indifference ... that way, at least, we don't have to change anything in our lives. God, however, can't be put in a "box" (unless that box is a tabernacle, but let's not digress).

A quick glance at Scripture reveals the exact opposite, actually. We do not have a cruel or indifferent or absent God — far from it. We have a God who not only loves us, *He likes us* and desires to spend time with us. Make no mistake, God the Father's goal is not intimidation, it is ***intimacy.***

In the previous reflection, we focused on God's reaction to Adam and Eve's sin, and His faithfulness in saving us even when our first parents were not faithful to Him. Do you know why God was there right after they interacted with the serpent and ate the fruit? They didn't call on Him. There was no divine "bat signal" shot into the sky to signal the Creator that there were problems in Paradise. No, God was out for a walk. That's right, God was taking a late afternoon/pre-sunset stroll in the garden of Eden. Pay attention to this beautiful and seemingly minuscule detail from Genesis, "And they heard the sound of the ***Lord God walking in***

the garden in the cool of the day, and the man and his wife hid themselves from the presence of the Lord God among the trees of the garden. But the Lord God called to the man, and said to him, "Where are you?" (Genesis 3:8-9, emphasis mine)

Notice that God was, again, not that distant Elohim but Yahweh, drawing near to them, completely accessible and friendly and desiring a relationship. God desires intimacy with His children. Note their response after sinning … we have the world's first game of hide and seek. Not much has really changed, to be honest. When we are doing well in our faith and praying and living the right way, we welcome God drawing near. Once we sin, though, and break the relationship and separate ourselves from God's love, we go silent, we hide and we avoid the Lord at all costs. God still desires intimacy with us, still today, but we — like Adam and Eve — are only open to it if we are in a good place spiritually and morally. Don't forget, though, that God being omniscient already knew what had happened. He didn't ask Adam where he was or what happened because He lacked the answer, He asked to help Adam live in truth of his own actions.

MAKING IT PERSONAL

It's been said that true love is spelled "t-i-m-e." In saying that God desired intimacy with us — that deep, personal connection — it infers that God wants time with us. He desires that connection to us, daily, which is why He teaches us to pray for our "daily bread." He wants us to develop a hunger for Him and a dependence on Him.

Does your daily life and schedule demonstrate a rhythm of prayer or do you pray sporadically, if at all? Today, set an alarm on your phone for every hour on the hour, or every two or three hours. When it goes off, stop and say a simple prayer inviting God into your day and life in a more intimate and intentional way.

DAY FIVE

Most people fall into two categories in life: those who are on time (usually early, actually) and those who are always late. It can cause serious frustration and strife — especially within families — when these different personality types are required to arrive somewhere together. Time is a gift from God but it has a funny way of feeling like a curse when the person you are traveling with does not share your same life philosophy or point of view.

When it comes to God's plan of salvation, it's vital to remember that although we are finite creatures — with a beginning and end — who function within space and time, God does not work that way. God is infinite; He has no beginning nor end. *God is timeless and life gets really tricky when we try to put the Timeless One on our timetable.* God works on His own schedule. Otherwise, He really wouldn't be God; He would be a sort of genie, a powerful being here solely to do our bidding. (Make no mistake, just because Jesus is the Light doesn't mean we can put Him in a lamp until we have a wish to fulfill.)

We see throughout the Old Testament a series of prophecies, many of which we hear about during the Advent season. Prophecies are promises and messages of God that come to fruition over a period of time according to God's plan and purpose. Go back and read Isaiah 7:14, Micah 5:2, Hosea 11:1, and Isaiah 60:6. The prophets who shared these messages usually did not even understand them, at least not fully. They were sharing what they were inspired by God to share but most of the prophets didn't even know each other or have access to one another. How amazing is it that all of the prophecies uttered by different people from different regions and different generations never even met? Yet all came true in one person: Jesus Christ.

Yes, God spoke through the prophets at different points in time and shed light on the coming of the Messiah (i.e., His identity, title, birthplace, and family tree). but God didn't give an exact date. His promise was unfolding over time according to His perfect plan, not our imperfect, short-sighted one.

Nothing has changed. We often still put God on our clock, asking and, even, expecting Him to work according to our schedule. God has never worked that way and never will. Rather than telling God when and how to act and frustrating ourselves, we would be wise to follow the example of the Blessed Virgin Mary and St. Joseph and all the saints ... place your prayers and fears before the Lord and trust that He will act in the appropriate way at the perfect time, according to His will.

MAKING IT PERSONAL

First, think of a time when you put limitations on God in prayer, asking for Him to answer an intention according to your desires rather than according to His will. Second, think of a situation you are currently praying about, struggling with, or hoping for a resolution to.

Now, learn from the first and apply it to the second. Say, "Father, I don't always understand you, but I trust you." Repeat the prayer as many times as you have to until you believe it or find peace. God's got this, just trust.

DAY SIX

For those of us born in the 20th and 21st centuries, it's hard for us to fully appreciate the deep and intense longing people experienced between the time of Genesis and the Incarnation. Every generation wondered if theirs would be the one who would finally lay eyes on Israel's Savior. As previously mentioned, prophecies gave clues as to where the Messiah would hail from or his lineage or what he would be like, but they were hard to understand. On top of that, the prophets were speaking at a difficult time in history, when God's people were oppressed, often ruled by bad and unrighteous kings and at war with or being enslaved by foreign powers.

That was the backdrop that the prophet, Jeremiah, was ministering within. When Jeremiah was called to preach truth and hope, the people were enslaved in a foreign land, their homes and temple had been destroyed and their future was dim. The people felt abandoned by God but He continued to assure them that He would make good on their promise and that hope was on the horizon. Though they were enslaved and immersed in darkness, God tried to breathe light through His young prophet, saying:

*"Behold, the days are coming, says the Lord, when I will make a new covenant ... **I will place my law within them,** and I will write it upon their hearts; and I will be their God, and they shall be my people ... for they shall all know me, from the least of them to the greatest, says the Lord; for I will forgive their iniquity, and I will remember their sin no more."* (Jeremiah 31:31, 33b-34, emphasis mine)

Now, there's no way that God's people understood what this meant. They had no idea what the "timeline" was for "the days [that were] coming." Little did they know it meant over 700 years later. Remember what we said about being patient and trusting God and not putting Him on the clock? What's even more amazing is did you catch what God said right in the middle (emphasized in bold)? He said His plan for the new covenant was to "place His law within them." In the Old

Covenant with Moses, He wrote His law (the Ten Commandments) on tablets of stone, externally for all to see. In the New Covenant (with Jesus) God is going to place the new Law (Jesus, Himself) *within us.* It will be an internal, intimate connection, not an external one.

Have you ever noticed that moment in the Catholic Mass during consecration when the priest utters the words, "Take this, all of you, and drink from it. For this is the chalice of my blood, the blood of **the new and eternal covenant**, which will be poured out for you..." Through the Incarnation, Jesus Christ — working through the person of the priest — is not only quoting St. Paul in 1 Corinthians 11:25, but He is fulfilling this prophecy from over 2,700 years ago.

For what could be more intimate than to have the body and blood of Jesus running through our veins after communion? Through Jeremiah, God promised that He would draw near and at every single Mass, in every single language, and in every corner of the world for 2,000 years. He has done just that.

MAKING IT PERSONAL

Consider the gift that the Eucharist is to you and to the Church. Now, consider what the Eucharist teaches us and tells us about God the Father.
He could look at us merely as sinners and say we are not worthy to have God draw near to us and dwell within us. He could come down merely to dwell in a tabernacle or monstrance. Instead, He makes us worthy by the blood of His cross, paying the debt we never could. He keeps us worthy by offering us a priesthood and the Sacrament of Confession to get us back into a state of grace, so we can receive Him worthily.

As St. Therese said, "For it is not to remain in a golden ciborium that He comes down each day from heaven. He comes to find another heaven, the heaven of our souls..." God's desire is not to remain in the ciborium (the golden dish that holds the Holy Eucharist), rather His desire is for us to become living tabernacles so that His light and life can draw near and shine forth for all to see.

DAY SEVEN

It's impossible to talk about the Incarnation — God taking flesh and becoming man — without mentioning one of the most significant moments in the history of time: the Annunciation. Really, it was at the Annunciation — when a messenger with incredible news visited a young teenage virgin in the village of Nazareth — that the Incarnation really "began," temporally speaking. As we have previously seen, God repeatedly used prophets century-after-century to deliver His news to the world. So, what prophet did God select to share the news with Mary that she was the one selected and preserved to carry and bear His only Son, the long-awaited Messiah? What was the prophet's name? Precisely. There was no prophet. No, for this news, God went to a much higher scale and sent an archangel, named Gabriel.

We usually rush past that part of the story when reading Luke's Gospel or praying the joyful mysteries of the rosary, but it's actually quite noteworthy. Why didn't God send a prophet to Nazareth on that fine spring day? Well, one reason God sent the Angel Gabriel is because the news Gabriel shared with the Blessed Virgin Mary had a cosmic significance. It was not only going to shake up things on Earth, her "yes" would rock both heaven and Earth. This moment would not only solidify Mary's role as the greatest saint but the Queen of Heaven and Earth!

God drew near to Mary in a unique and life-altering way ... and the life that was altered was not merely hers, but yours and mine and everyone else's throughout human history. An angel of light visited an anonymous and open-hearted teenager from a tiny town and darkness was forever vanquished. Consider how special the Virgin Mary is to all three persons of the Trinity. How she was elevated and kept from original sin by God the Father. How she held and raised and loved her Son, Jesus. How incredible a connection she had with the Holy Spirit. And this is the soul that Jesus gifted to us all from the cross, proclaiming to His beloved disciple, John, that she is now our mother, too. The Queen of the Angels — the only human greater than the angels — is your mother. It's yet another way that God draws near to us, making His favorite daughter and mother available to pray with us and for us, every day.

MAKING IT PERSONAL

Say a prayer and ask the Lord Jesus to give you a greater love for Mary. Pray that you would have a love for Mary like He has, and a respect for Mary like He has, that you could honor Mary like He does and have a heart for His mother like He does.

For us to truly appreciate the wonder of the Incarnation in all its fullness, we must pause to reflect on the soul through whom God made it possible.

DAY EIGHT

So much happens during the Mass — so many little movements and moments that might not even catch our attention but are, actually, very meaningful — times we stand and times we kneel, times we bow and times we join together in a chorus. Every moment means "something" but oftentimes we may not stop to consider what exactly they mean.

The Church — in her wisdom — is trying to teach us something far more than Catholic calisthenics. Like a good mother, the Church is trying to get us to lean in, to engage, and to pay attention to what is unfolding in the sanctuary, in front of our very eyes. By invoking and involving our bodies and voices, these movements are supposed to draw us and our attention more fully into the Mass.

A particular "little moment" of Mass that holds great significance is when the priest prays over the gifts. It's part of what's called the *consecration* (which is Latin for "to dedicate and make sacred"). In that particular moment, the priest stands behind the altar and brings his hands down in sort of a large sweeping motion over the bread and wine. This movement — called the *epiclesis* (Greek for "to call down") — is when the priest prays and asks the Holy Spirit to come over the gifts and transform them from mere bread and wine into the very precious Body, Blood, Soul, and Divinity of Jesus, Himself. Even if one's mind wanders in that moment and you don't hear or listen to the words, the over exaggerated and sweeping movement of the arms and hands over the gifts ought to cause even the tuned-out attendee at Mass to stop and stare into the sanctuary. What's amazing, though, is that this is not just some random, prayerful "gesture" that the Church made up a few hundred years ago. This epiclesis moment has its roots in Sacred Scripture.

Remember when the Archangel Gabriel visited the Virgin Mary for the Annunciation? She asked "how can this be" that she could bear a son without having relations with a man? The angel assured Mary that the Holy Spirit of God would "overshadow" her — that the Spirit would come down upon her. At every single Mass, when the priest makes that sweeping gesture with his hands over the gifts of bread and wine, the Holy Spirit transforms them into the very body and blood of Jesus Christ. The same Spirit who brought life in Nazareth is bringing Nazareth to your local parish every Sunday. It's as though, at every Mass, we are entering into the Annunciation all over again. Every Mass is — in a way — Christmas and Easter, when the Lord is both made present and offered for our sins. This great mystery is so deep yet so simple and the Church gives us this great movement and moment within the Mass to remind us of the timeless truth of what happened when God drew near and took flesh so many centuries ago. He is still drawing near through the power of His priesthood at every single Mass.

MAKING IT PERSONAL

There are so many nonverbal ways we communicate good and bad things. A smile can literally change someone else's day. So can a roll of the eyes. The epiclesis is a nonverbal sign that God is present with us.

Today, find ways to nonverbally share Christ with someone. Smile and wave. Grin and nod. God gave you a smile for a reason; use it.

DAY NINE

It's amazing what, in life, we put our time and energy into. Some people are passionate about working out, others about sports, still others about food or music or reading. Some souls rise and fall with the stock market and growing their wealth while others focus on their looks. Regardless, when someone is passionate about something (or someone) it normally shows in their conversations, behavior, and overall approach to life.

One of the most profound moments we read about the Incarnation is an often overlooked line in St. Luke's Gospel. It speaks to both Mary's posture of heart at the time and our own ongoing responsibility to the Gospel message entrusted to us. We can read about it following the Annunciation in Luke chapter one: *"In those days Mary arose and **went with haste** into the hill country, to a city of Judah and she entered the* *house of Zechariah and greeted Elizabeth."* (Luke 1:39-40, emphasis mine)

What was the last thing that inspired you so much that you went "with haste" to share it with someone? Was it a great meal at a new restaurant? Was it an incredible movie? Perhaps it was a song you loved or a YouTube video you thought was hilarious. Regardless, when something really inspires us, we feel the need to share about it far and wide, right? That is why Mary went *in haste* to the hill country to see her cousin. She had news about a person (Jesus) that she just had to share.

Have you ever been *that excited* to share about Jesus?

MAKING IT PERSONAL

When and where do you share about your relationship with Jesus? Perhaps you do it often — with everyone you come into contact with. Maybe you share on social media. If so, were the souls you shared Him with receptive to what you had to say?

If you have not shared about Jesus, why not share about Him? Is it embarrassment or fear of what someone might say or think? Is it an anxiety of how someone might not look at you the same again after you "out yourself" as a follower of the Lord?

Today, take 60 seconds to share about your relationship with God either on social media or in conversation. Have a sense of urgency and boldness like the Blessed Virgin had. Just ask the Holy Spirit for guidance on when, where, and how to share. And, then, be bold!

DAY TEN

Daily, her belly grew. For nine months, God's only Son dwelt within Mary's womb — the world's first tabernacle. With every passing week, the Light of the World became more visible. The Lord was certainly drawing near over those three trimesters. Imagine Mary's anticipation. They had waited centuries upon centuries for the promised Messiah and now they actually had a timetable and a "due date" (so to speak). Of course, a time of preparation was necessary. The God of the universe was not merely "announced" before showing up on some cloud. No, God knew that Mary (and Joseph) and the world needed time to prepare for what was — at that moment — the most important event in the history of the world.

Mary was fully present to God's divine presence within her. Though she was assuredly excited to meet her son and hold Him for the first time, Mary — being the perfect disciple and a picture of virtue

— undoubtedly saw the time of her pregnancy as a gift to behold. The nine months would not have been seen as an annoying precursor but, instead, as a valuable time of reflection.

In the same way, the season of Advent is not merely some temporal formality we are forced to endure each year, it is supposed to be a gift. The Church could have done away with the season of Advent altogether and just decided to throw Jesus a birthday party every year when Christmas rolls around. Wisely, mother Church sees the bigger picture. The very word "Advent" means "the coming" or "the arrival." In setting aside four weeks before we celebrate the Incarnation, the Church invites us — like Mary — to behold the mystery that's about to unfold. Consider the Advent wreath and the four candles we light with each consecutive week. Slowly we add more and more light until ... what? Until the light overpowers the darkness. As we draw closer to Christmas, just as Mary drew closer to childbirth (and to Bethlehem), Jesus — the Light of life — is coming and darkness "could not comprehend it." (John 1:5)

MAKING IT PERSONAL

Light your Advent wreath today and make it a point to light it every day, if you can. If you don't have one, make it your goal to buy or make one in the coming days. When you light it, don't do it mindlessly but really try to enter into the moment. Watch as the flame ignites and how light casts out darkness. Try to add candles — votives or full size, real or battery powered — throughout your room or home. Remind yourself not only of the impending Christmas season, but of the reality of the need to wait in eager anticipation, daily, for the coming of the Lord.

DAY ELEVEN

Imagine being torn between two good things. Do I choose the milkshake or the ice cream sundae? Do I go with the buffalo wings or the cheeseburger? Is it better to take a long nap on the couch or sleep in my own bed? Would I rather watch my team win in a blowout or watch my least favorite team lose in a heartbreaker?

While none of these are life-changing ... it's hard to live with such choices when both offer a good ending. These scenarios — as stupid as they may be — force us out of indecision. When trying to pick the "right" answer (which is obviously subjective in these examples), it challenges us to focus objectively, answering as honestly as possible. In answering these questions (and the ones in life which get FAR harder), it reveals what or who guides our decision making and why we choose the outcomes that we do.

Consider the dilemma faced by St. Joseph when he learned about Mary's pregnancy. They were betrothed — which included the legal ramifications of marriage — even though they had not yet professed their final vows or lived together. Saint Joseph is described in Scripture as a deeply righteous man, who obviously had a profound love and respect for God. At the same time, Joseph deeply loved Mary and although the news of her pregnancy must have shocked and confounded him, he was "unwilling to expose her to shame" (Matthew 1:19), for news of this apparent infidelity could lead to her being legally stoned to death.

Saint Joseph was faced with a terrible situation. As badly as he wanted to honor the law of God, he also wanted to honor his bride. One doesn't need a great empathy to understand Joseph's obvious anguish. Likely in emotional torment, Joseph no doubt prayed hard for God's wisdom and guidance. Fatigued from the work and stress of the day, Joseph fell asleep ... *and God drew near.*

At God's command, "an angel of the Lord appeared to him in a dream, saying 'Joseph, son of David, do not fear to take Mary as your wife, for that which is conceived in her is of the Holy Spirit.'" (Matthew 1:20) Consider the love and mercy of God in this moment. He knew his righteous son was confused and stressed, crying out in prayer and God sent an angel to console him. In fact, this is the first of three times God spoke to Joseph through an angelic dream intervention. In these examples, we see just how deeply God loved St. Joseph and, by extension, all of us. We might think that our stresses don't matter to God or that He is somehow "too busy" to care about little old us. Nothing could be further from the truth. When we pray, God listens (Jeremiah 29:12) and, when necessary, He intervenes ... oftentimes in unexpected ways.

MAKING IT PERSONAL

Write out a list of all the situations or relationships that are currently causing you stress or anxiety. Now, invite St. Joseph to pray with you and for you so that you may lay those stresses at the feet of the Lord. And whenever you feel like you are facing an impossible situation or you are in over your head, reach out to St. Joseph. He's been there and will continue to be there to intercede for you.

DAY TWELVE

By now in the Advent season everyone has likely heard the hymn "O Come, O Come, Emmanuel" at least a dozen times ... performed by everyone from Pentatonix to Lauren Daigle. It's easy when a song is so well known to allow the depth of the lyrics to escape you. Though the song is only about 150 years old, the prophecy of the coming Emmanuel was spoken by Isaiah over 2,700 years ago with the words, "The Lord Himself will give you a sign. Behold, a young virgin will conceive and bear a son, and shall call him Immanuel." (Isaiah 7:14)

Sadly, though, even the most beautiful and commonly known Christmas songs can become like white noise to the soul during the days leading up to the Savior's birth. Consider the lyrics, for a moment and look upon them with fresh eyes:

O come, O come, Emmanuel,
And ransom captive Israel
That mourns in lonely exile here
Until the Son of God appears
Rejoice! Rejoice! Emmanuel
Shall come to thee, O Israel.

The children of God laid in wait, breathless with anticipation of the promised Messiah. Age after age, they yearned for God to fulfill His promise and the prophecy to come true. Over the centuries, Israel (who was God's firstborn "child") had been overrun by various kingdoms and enemy forces. Whether the Egyptians or the Philistines, the Babylonians or Assyrians, the Persians or the Greeks, the Israelites were constantly overrun by foreign world powers. It wasn't until they were oppressed by Roman rule that God fulfilled the prophecy. In Jesus, God drew near to "ransom captive Israel" once and for all. Century after century Israel mourned and feared for the Son of God to appear. When you listen to the song, hear and feel the yearning from God's people.

We are told by St. Matthew that Emmanuel means "God with us" (Matthew 1:23). It's less of a formal name and more of a reminder that even in times of darkness (like Isaiah was living in) that

God does not abandon us, ever. It foreshadows the final words in this Gospel, too, when Christ reminds us that He will "be with us always, until the end of the age." (Matthew 28:20)

MAKING IT PERSONAL

Think of a time that you felt distant from God or, more to the point, you felt He was distant from you. Ponder a moment when you called out to God in prayer to come to your aid, to be with you, or to rescue you from sin or loneliness or pain or suffering. Then find a version of the song you can really pray with. By virtue of your Baptism you, like Israel, are God's child. He cares for you *and* about you. He is there for you, always. And like any good parent, He wants you to come to Him — to call out to Him (in speech or song) — when your heart is troubled or lonely.

DAY THIRTEEN

Have you ever said or done something without thinking about how it affects other people? Perhaps you were mad at a family member or friend and overreacted. Maybe you make a decision without having all the facts, and later found out your decision had a negative affect on others. Of course, we don't always know or see how our actions or words can impact others. That is why we must seek God in all things and trust in His providence and perfect plan.

Two thousand years ago, the Roman Emperor — one of the most powerful men at the time — lifted his finger and ordered a census. The Jewish people were ordered to return to their towns of family origin and in the ninth month of pregnancy, a young bride and her new husband were forced to travel 90 miles south to the husband's ancestral birthplace. As the song reminds us, it was a little town called "Bethlehem," which means "house of bread." There could be no more appropriate place for the Bread of Life to hail from, assuredly, but there is no chance that the Prophet Micah could conceive of Jesus' future title when he penned the prophecy over 700 years before that holy night at the manger. Micah pinpoints the location of the Messiah's birth (5:2) but he never could have known of the census that drove the holy couple from Nazareth there.

Bethlehem was the hometown and birthplace of Joseph's ancestor, David. Given that Joseph took Jesus in as his own Son, He was considered "from the line of David." Of course, David was both shepherd and, later, king ... and Jesus, the Good Shepherd and King of Kings would follow in His footsteps. Mary and Joseph likely knew Micah's prophecy and the story of King David. Imagine what their conversation may have sounded like on their four-to-five day walk. How their hearts and minds must have been overwhelmed — not with anger over the journey but with God's creative plan unfolding before their very eyes.

MAKING IT PERSONAL

Think about all the things in your life — from where you were born, to where you live, to the people you know. Consider that these places and relationships you were born into or developed over time did not happen by chance but, rather, from God's providence. Thank God for His perfect plan — even if you don't understand it. And, the next time something doesn't go your way, or you are frustrated by someone else's decision, try to imitate the Holy Family and trust that God can use every challenge for His glory.

DAY FOURTEEN

There are several villains in the Bible. Satan (obviously), Goliath, Jezebel, and Judas Iscariot just to name a few others. And then there are characters who people have rolled their eyes at for centuries but who, truthfully, didn't deserve the disrespect.

We mock Martha for being so busy serving Jesus that she didn't sit at His feet like her sister Mary. Think about it — she was *serving Jesus*, yet she gets made fun of by many. Then there's St. Thomas who we refer to most often as "Doubting Thomas" because he missed the apostolic staff meeting on Easter night and couldn't believe his ears when he heard about the Resurrection. He will forever be associated with his doubt when it was really just disbelief that something so amazing happened. He loved the Lord and followed Him with abandon ... not exactly worthy of mockery, but mocked Tommy will be.

One of the characters who I've never understood getting a bad rap in the Bible is a nameless innkeeper ... who doesn't even speak! We are reminded every Christmas that Mary and Joseph were turned away in Bethlehem "because there was no room in the inn." (Luke 2:7) We think to ourselves "what a heartless monger, turning away a pregnant woman in labor." But if the rooms were occupied, was he supposed to just evict someone else and throw them out onto Bethlehem's streets? Can you imagine Jesus coming into the world in a room that evicted someone else? It wouldn't be the nicest start for the God of mercy, right? No, the innkeeper did his job and Jesus was able to be birthed in a cave and laid in a manger.

We are told not to be like the innkeeper and to "make space" in our hearts for the Lord to dwell there. But God *made space* for His Son to be born. He took care of His own. It may not have been what they wanted, but it fulfilled what they needed. That is a trustworthy Father.

MAKING IT PERSONAL

Look around your home or bedroom. Peer into your closet, desk or dresser. Identify what you want and what you "need." What can you give away this Advent season that will help the less fortunate? How can you "make room" in your inn and declutter your life a bit? How can you provide for another's needs like God did for the Holy Family?

DAY FIFTEEN

My last reflection may have sounded strange — to hear me praise God for allowing His only Son, the blessed Virgin Mary, and St. Joseph to use a cave, full of stabled animals, for the most important delivery room in the history of creation. So, why, exactly would God allow that? To teach us a lesson about His great and unparalleled humility? To demonstrate the holy couple's incredible trust and gratitude? To foreshadow Christ as the true and eternal food (Eucharist) by placing Him in a feed box? All seem plausible. But, maybe it was to fulfill yet another Old Testament prophecy from Isaiah: "The ox knows its owner, and the ass its master's manger; but Israel does not know, my people do not understand." (Isaiah 1:3)

This is yet another one of those prophecies that the prophet, himself, could never have fathomed the true meaning of. Yes, Israel did not understand what God was doing at the time, just as Mary and Joseph didn't understand God's plan. The difference is that the people in Isaiah's time had stopped worshiping and trusting the Lord. Jesus' parents obviously didn't struggle with that problem.

You likely have a nativity set in your home and most definitely at your local parish. Have you ever wondered why the ox and the ass (a.k.a. the donkey) appear in virtually every nativity set? They are not mentioned anywhere in the Gospel accounts of the nativity. No animals are, really, only the mention of the manger that animals would eat from. The actual reason these beasts of burden appear in nativity sets is precisely this prophecy from Isaiah. It's a valuable prayer practice to really ponder the nativity scene and meditate on it — so valuable that when St. Francis of Assisi gave the world its first nativity set (called "the creche") he did it to help people draw nearer to the God who drew near to us.

Before 1223, most people celebrated Christmas by going to Mass in Latin, a language few people spoke. Some churches would feature beautiful artwork of the Child Jesus, but St. Francis wanted to think bigger. He wanted to make the story of the Holy Family more accessible to ordinary people and so after a Christmas Eve Mass in December 1223, he found a small cave outside of Greccio, Italy, where he enlisted people to play the roles of Mary and Joseph while cradling a wax figure of the baby Jesus. He invited local shepherds and their sheep. He also loaned a live donkey and a live ox from a local farmer for the scene.

Perhaps the simplest and most profound "lesson" we can learn from God allowing His only Son to be born amidst the animals — with a manger for a crib — is that, put simply, God is not afraid of our mess. We sometimes make the mistake of thinking we need to be perfect or act perfectly for God to love us, but that would make God's love conditional and imperfect. No, the God of the universe emptied Himself and took on flesh — coming into the world amongst the dirt and filth of the cave of the nativity — proving that God is not afraid of our mess(es). We don't have to live in shame. We have a God who drew near amidst the messy animals and filthy stable. In turn, He is unflinching about the mess of our lives. We need not be ashamed to invite God in and trust that He will make Himself at home.

MAKING IT PERSONAL

Ponder the nativity scene, once again. Look at the cast of characters and animals. Who do you most relate to? Do you feel intimately close to Jesus like Mary? Do you feel the need to protect and defend Him and the faith, like Joseph? Do you tell others of Him like the angels? Are you stubborn like the donkey or thick-headed like the ox? Really spend time putting yourself into the mind of each character and you will soon see why St. Francis' idea was so inspired.

DAY SIXTEEN

The God of heaven coming to Earth? A virgin birth? Angelic dream interventions? A third trimester road trip? A baby born between animals? A feed box used for a crib? God the Father certainly is unpredictable; our Lord does not lack creativity. In fact, the Bible teaches us, book after book and chapter after chapter that God doesn't think or act or move like we do. He is purposeful and intentional.

One of the most important questions that atheists, agnostics, and doubters must wrestle with is "if there is a God, **could** He do x, y, z..." Oftentimes, people (even believers) say, "Well, would God really do that?" But that's the wrong question. When we ask that question, we are putting ourselves on God's intellectual plain. We assume that God thinks like us which, again, He clearly does not. No, the question we need to ask is not "would God do that" but, instead "**could**

God do it?" When it comes to the Eucharist, it doesn't logically make sense at first hearing why the God of heaven and Earth would humble Himself and allow His divine presence to dwell in a piece of bread. But that is where we lose sight of the bigger picture. It's not about whether or not God would do it this way, it's about whether the God of the universe — who multiplied the loaves and walked on water and healed the blind and raised the dead — *could* offer His flesh and blood in the Eucharist.

The Eucharist was not a "last minute idea" God came up with on Holy Thursday. No, remember the earlier prophecy from Jeremiah. He foretold that He would place His law "within us." In this way, Mary's room was the first tabernacle and the manger a monstrance. The journey to Bethlehem was a eucharistic procession, of sorts, and the visitors to the manger were the first to attend Eucharistic Adoration beside the Holy Family.

The baby in the manger proves to us that God comes to us in unexpected and surprising ways ... just like the Eucharist. You may not, initially, recognize the Lord in the sacred host, but give it time. If the people of Nazareth taught us anything during Jesus' life, they taught us this: the God of the universe could be truly present right in front of you and you might not recognize Him.

MAKING IT PERSONAL

Try to go to Adoration in your parish today or this week. If there is no Adoration chapel or time set up for Adoration, it's OK, just go and sit in the church (when Mass is not going on).

Ponder the tabernacle. Focus on it. Christ's true presence is within. Go and sit with Him and worship the God of creativity, who figured out a way to truly be Emmanuel — God with us — even after Jesus died on the cross. He is accessible in every parish in every corner of the world, fulfilling His promise never to leave us.

DAY SEVENTEEN

What did it sound like when the baby Jesus laughed? How big were His eyes? Did He have dimples? Did He enter the world with a thick head of hair? What did His cry sound like? What did it feel like for Mary to kiss the forehead of the one who created the moon and the stars ... even the very star of Bethlehem? How scared was Joseph to hold the God of the Universe in his splintered carpenter's hands?

If you were there, would you want to hold Him or would you feel too unworthy and scared? Would you kiss His brow or take a step back, just thankful to be on such holy ground? There is no right answer, but your answer does reveal how personal and intimate you consider your relationship with the Messiah right now in your life.

It might seem like a crazy idea — God inviting you to the deliverer's delivery but that's what He does at every single Mass and during Eucharistic Adoration. God is gazing at you, He's asking you, inviting you, begging you to take a second look and see beyond the appearance of bread. He's asking you in prayer to imagine His face — the face of God — staring back at you. This level of contemplation is a great exercise for the spiritual life. The more we can enter into the greatest story ever told, the more the God of life will be seen, felt, and heard in our lives.

Whether you are comfortable around babies or not, whether you're a parent or not — babies bring the best out of people through their fragility and gentleness. God chose to enter the world dependent on His parents. He chose to be vulnerable and accessible. God did the unthinkable and unimaginable and drew near as a baby boy. On that silent night, a baby's cry rang out for the first time and in that instant, history was forever changed.

MAKING IT PERSONAL

Picture the baby Jesus in Mary's arms. Really try to imagine what He looked like, how she held Him and the entire setting. Imagine yourself there in the first hour after Jesus was born. Look at the animals. Pay attention to the details of the scene all the way down to the hay in the manger. The more you can enter into the scene, the better you will understand and appreciate what God did for us all that historic night in Bethlehem.

DAY EIGHTEEN

Have you ever seen an angel up close? Once in a while in Scripture, we get a description of angels drawing near to people in "human disguise" — but, this is usually quite rare. Typically angels appear, instead, in all their light and majesty, and end up having to tell the people they appear before "not to fear." Why does this happen do you suppose? Most likely because an angel's appearance and power — all emanating from the one, true God — is so radiant and overwhelming the human heart doesn't know whether to run, bow, or stare.

According to the teachings of St. Thomas Aquinas, there are nine different "levels" (called choirs) of angels, all with different jobs or functions. Some angels serve as messengers (the word "angel," in fact, actually meaning messenger). So, when God sends angels with a message, as He did with the blessed Virgin Mary, it's His way of saying something is a pretty big deal.

Imagine, now, that you are a shepherd keeping watch over the flock at night. You're minding your own business. Possibly fighting off sleep because a sleeping shepherd equals dead sheep. Your eyes are heavy, the sheep are sleeping, and you are huddling to stay warm when — out of the blue — the darkened Bethlehem sky fills with light. There's a sound like rushing wind and thunder. You look up and see an angel announcing to you that "a Savior has been born in the city of David, who is Christ the Lord." (Luke 2:11) You're told the baby will be lying in a manger. (Luke 2:12) Your mouth gapes open. Your eyes are mesmerized. You can't believe what you're actually hearing and, then ... God takes it up a notch.

In his Gospel, St. Luke tells us (at that point) "... suddenly there was with the angel a multitude of the heavenly host praising God and saying, 'Glory to God in the highest, and on Earth peace among men with whom He is pleased.'" (Luke 2:13-14). At that moment, heaven came to Earth to announce *that heaven had come to Earth.* God had not just drawn near via angels; He became man. This eruption of the heavenly host — of dozens, possibly even hundreds of angels — filling the sky with their radiance and the air with their singing is why we sing "Glory to God in the highest" at

Mass. We sing these lines to join our voices to the heavenly host in praising the presence of God coming into our midst.

MAKING IT PERSONAL

Ask your guardian angel to pray with you today and in the days moving forward. To get into the habit, set several alarms on your phone in the morning that will go off throughout the day. Whenever one rings, stop and invite your guardian angel to be with you, to pray for you, to protect and to guide you. If you don't know it, learn the guardian angel prayer and commit it to memory:

Angel of God, my guardian dear, to whom God's love commits me here,
ever this day be at my side, to light and guard, to rule and guide.

DAY NINETEEN

Have you ever felt forgotten, ignored, or — worse yet — purposely left out of something? Maybe there was a party you heard about but were not invited to attend. Perhaps you were the last to get picked for a team or had to eat lunch alone at a new school or job. Maybe people have pretended not to see or hear you because they seemed uninterested that you were there. Whatever the scenario, it can hurt deeply to feel invisible or be treated like you don't matter.

In the last entry, we took a closer look at the angelic birth announcement to the shepherds watching over their flocks on Bethlehem's hills. We may see the characters in the nativity set or hear about them in the story, but rarely do we spend time talking about them. Why did God announce His Son's birth to the shepherds of all people? Why not the townspeople? Why not the more influential or important people or, possibly, someone who could help protect the Holy Family from a homicidal king? God's inclusion of the shepherds may seem like a minor thing to those of us in the 21st century but it would have been shocking to the people in Jesus' day.

Shepherds were not exactly "A-list" celebrities back then; they were not "influencers" in any sense of the word. Shepherds often had a bad reputation, actually. Often uneducated, unbathed and disrespected, shepherds were not accustomed to being on people's birthday party guest list, and certainly not commonly seen at a baby shower. These were guys who spent a majority of time with sheep and probably smelled like it. The angels' announcement would likely have seemed odd even to them. Even though Moses and David both served as shepherds at one point in their lives, it was not normally seen as a noble trade for the important and influential. Good shepherds — as Jesus points out later in His ministry — are noble and courageous and hard to come by, yes. But, oftentimes shepherds were just hired hands, in it for the money, and not willing to lay down their lives for their sheep.

God's inclusion of the shepherds into this historic and sacred moment sends a message to all of us that Jesus is *for all of us.* We may be forgotten or ignored by others or by the world. We may not "have it all together." We might be a mess in the eyes of many, undesirable, or "unimportant" but God still includes us in His story. He sees us, loves us, and is inviting us into a deeper relationship with Him. Imagine how validated and special the shepherds felt that night. How affirmed they were. How amazed at God's mercy to include them into such an amazing moment. Now, consider how amazing it is that as God still draws near at every Mass, He invites you and I to know and receive Him in the Eucharist. He doesn't ignore us because we are messy; He loves us *because we are.*

MAKING IT PERSONAL

Consider the people in your life. Is there anyone you need to be nicer to? Is there anyone you need to ask forgiveness from for how you've treated them? Is there anyone you need to forgive for how they've treated you? Pray for the courage and strength to forgive and to ask for forgiveness where necessary. Look around for the "shepherds" in your life and offer them the love of Christ, today.

DAY TWENTY

Have you ever met a "big time" celebrity? Maybe you spotted a famous actor or actress in an airport or got an autograph from a well-known athlete. Perhaps you got a selfie with a famous musician or shook hands with a big-name star. If you haven't, imagine how you'd feel if someone you really looked up to or admired all of a sudden was face-to-face with you. It'd be a day you would never forget. Would you feel excited? Commit the moment to your memory? Take 100 selfies? Refuse to wash your hands ever again? Would you be "overjoyed"? Would your joy reach excessive levels you've never experienced?

The magi were excited when they saw a star, too, but for very different reasons. The star they beheld was one filled with both promise and mystery. The heavenly orb led them to an even greater heavenly reality in a manger. The Prophet Isaiah told us this would happen, but it was the

Gentiles (non-Jews) who cracked this code. They didn't just look for the star, they actually had the courage to follow it. Their journey would have taken weeks ... months, in fact. This was not a day trip or a weekend getaway. No, the magi were committed. They would have had to pack heavy bags (well beyond the three gifts). They were likely tired, but they kept moving forward and stopped at nothing. They had to see this promised King for themselves, with their own eyes.

Their arrival and imminent worship did more than reveal the baby's royal identity; it revealed God's long-standing and amazing plan to save us. Jesus was coming for everyone (Gentiles included), not just the "chosen" Jewish people.

Did you catch that? The wise men thought they were seeking the Lord only to realize that the God of the universe (not even "their" god) was actually the one seeking *them*! We are all invited to behold this mystery, to contemplate it, and to celebrate it.

MAKING IT PERSONAL

How far are you willing to go for God? The magi went to extremes to be in the presence of God.

We often complain about having to get out of bed or fast from food for an hour before Mass. This week, go above and beyond for God. Head to a daily Mass if you can. Stop by the chapel on a day other than Sunday. Dress nicer for Mass than usual and show up early so you can really pray and prepare your heart for the Lord. Be like the magi and go a step beyond what others would do.

DAY TWENTY-ONE

About 12 days after Christmas, we celebrate the Feast of the Epiphany. Focusing on the events following Christ's birth, we celebrate the day the magi arrived and worshiped the King of Kings. While they didn't RSVP for this baby shower, it's difficult to imagine Mary or Joseph would have complained — especially when they carried in the gifts they did; gold, frankincense, and myrrh weren't cheap (and not easily purchased from their local Target). When the "wise men" parked their camels and fell on their knees, their act of worship revealed something amazing — good news that would impact us all.

Saint Matthew details the encounter for us in chapter two of his Gospel:

"When they had heard the king they went their way; and lo, the star which they had seen in the East went before them, till it came to rest over

the place where the child was. When they saw the star, they rejoiced exceedingly with great joy; and going into the house they saw the child with Mary, His mother, and they fell down and worshiped Him. Then, opening their treasures, they offered Him gifts, gold and frankincense and myrrh." (Matthew 2:9-11)

Envision this miraculous encounter. The star they'd followed now came to rest, the light shining in darkness now showered light upon the Light of the World. God from God, light from light, true God from true God. Here lay a baby — born and begotten, though not made — so radiant in splendor that the hearts of learned minds became so full, they fell to their knees. They understood full well that God had, indeed, drawn near. Picture Mary's expression at this moment. They all knew the prophecy, but Mary held the prophet. The shepherds had come and found the Lamb (of God) ... now the wise men came and found Wisdom in the flesh.

Think about what the magi demonstrated. Just as God offers us His physical presence (in Christ, Jesus), we are invited to offer ourselves back to Him as they did, along with our gifts and talents.

A gift is not a gift until it is freely given ... until then it is a possession.

MAKING IT PERSONAL

Make a list of your talents. This is not a time to play overly humble. Everyone has different gifts and talents and skills that make them unique. What has God blessed you with and created you to do and be? Now, how have you used them for His glory? We must not forget the simplest lessons the magi taught us: they showed up, brought their gifts, and worshiped the Lord. Ask yourself, do I do all three? If not ... "Why?" And if so, keep it up.

DAY TWENTY-TWO

How and where we spend our time and energy says a lot about us. Consider your day like it's a pie chart. Where does your time go? How much time is spent sleeping, eating, working, or scrolling through social media. How big of a slice on this pie is your prayer life, currently? What areas have grown unbalanced or out of proportion?

At the end of the last reflection, we saw that the magi showed up, brought their gifts, and worshiped the Lord. That third piece — worshiping the Lord — cannot be glossed over too quickly, yet it often is. The magi were not Jewish and had no "obligation" to worship Him (let alone travel that far to see Him). They spent their time and energy seeking God and kneeling before Him. Again, in their simple example is a profound lesson about life and the right order we should seek to live in.

Do you worship the Lord with all your heart, mind, soul, and strength as God asks and commands us to do? Do you make it to Mass and Confession regularly? Is time with God a priority each day? Have you allowed any other things in your life to take precedence or push God out of His rightful spot within the manger of your heart?

MAKING IT PERSONAL

If you are willing, take some time to pray now. Ask God to reveal to you what people or things, fears or stresses may have inadvertently become your "god." You may want to compile a list of the things that occupy a majority of your thoughts instead of God. What are the stresses that render you distant when you're called to be present to family or friends? What are the anxieties that steal your focus and energy when you go to pray?

If you aren't sure "who your God is" you might want to begin with your social media profile. Who and what do you post about the most? Who occupies a majority of your thoughts and energy? If Christ was right (and He always is) when He said, "where your treasure is, there your heart is, also" (Matthew 6:21), then we can learn a lot from where we spend our time and energy. We cannot worship the true God until we acknowledge any false gods that have crept in and set up shop in our lives, homes, schedules, and souls.

DAY TWENTY-THREE

Sometimes we get so caught up in the joy of Christmas that we forget "the rest of the story." It was an amazing moment when God became man, but that doesn't mean that the Holy Family had it easy. Far from it. We can't forget that the Magi had encountered King Herod — who wanted to know the whereabouts of the newborn Christ child. Threatened by ancient prophecies coming true, the bloodthirsty king wanted the baby dead. God had raised a star in the heavens, magi had traveled, Mary and Joseph had too, the inn was full, the angels had proclaimed, the shepherds visited and just when things were supposed to calm down, it got even more dangerous. It took angelic intervention of a sleeping St. Joseph to flee the town under the veil of night — escaping the grip of a homicidal king. It took the magi leaving by a different route to avoid Herod. Over the months and years that followed, the Holy Family and the blessed magi assuredly processed all they had experienced. What an unbelievable turn of events.

This is no Disney movie, though. This is not the "happy ending" to the birth story. This is reality. This happened. This was another miraculous event in the historic battle between good and evil — where the light, once again, overcame the darkness. These were real souls that journeyed, worshiped, adored, and eventually returned home, changed forever. During the Epiphany, the epic saga of salvation history takes a dramatic and unexpected turn, announcing God's presence to a world desperately in need of it. Nothing much has changed. You are like the magi now, traveling to your local Bethlehem (your parish), advancing toward a different looking manger (the altar), and laying down your gifts and your life before the King each week. You kneel. You worship. But will you, like the magi, allow the Lord to change you forever?

In the end, all three magi became saints of the Catholic Church. That's what encountering Jesus and worshiping Him can do. Will people be celebrating your life 2,000 years from now? Will you become a saint? If your immediate response to that last sentence was, "Me? A saint? Not a chance!" then may I submit your God is too small. No sin is greater than His mercy ... no sin. God took flesh to save us from our sins. He gave us His Holy Spirit to help us become saints. The Holy Spirit's job is — quite literally — to make us holy. You getting to heaven: that's the goal and the happiest possible ending to life.

MAKING IT PERSONAL

Write out all the excuses you may have or reasons you think you could not become a saint. Next, share them with God. Ask the Holy Spirit to reveal to you what areas of your life are holding you back from sainthood and any things you may need to leave behind to truly be the holiest version of yourself that you can be.

DAY TWENTY-FOUR

At first glance, the Joyful Mysteries might not appear that joyful. Consider these moments from the Gospel: a teenage virgin is pregnant but not with her husband's child. The girl then leaves home for three months and later travels 90 miles by donkey in her third trimester of pregnancy. She then gives birth in a cave surrounded by animals, hears from a prophet that both she and her child will suffer greatly, and then, to top it all off, she and her husband have their pre-teen son ... the son of God ... go missing for three days.

Most would not consider these moments very joyful. Upon further reflection on these mysterious events, however, you begin to see that they are *actually* a cause for intense joy. God was on a rescue mission to save you, and that mission included some courageous souls fighting through some incredibly challenging and painful situations. Not only do the Joyful Mysteries walk us more deeply into the conception, birth, and childhood of our Lord Jesus, they reveal to us a God who is madly in love with us ... a God who will stop at nothing to save all of us from death.

There's a famous saying that "in order to be successful you should 'begin with the end in mind.'" If that is the case, there is no better example of "success" than the Gospels. God, quite obviously, had a detailed plan to save us, as the birth and the death of Jesus have striking similarities.

Consider just these few parallels between Bethlehem and Calvary:

- Angels are present during Jesus' birth, death, and Resurrection. (Luke 2:13; Matthew 26:53; John 20:12)
- Mary, our mother, is present in both accounts. (Matthew 2:11-13; John 19:26-27)
- In both scenes, Jesus was draped in swaddling clothes. (Luke 2:7, 23:53)
- Each event was accompanied by a celestial act/sign. (Matthew 2:2, 27:45)
- The wooden manger lies between two animals, the wooden cross between two thieves. (Isaiah 1:3; Luke 2:12, 23:33)

- A righteous man named Joseph was present at both His birth and His death. (Luke 2:16; 19:38)
- Jesus was pronounced "King of the Jews" at each. (Matthew 2:2; John 19:19)

Both events took place on a hill, on the outskirts of Jerusalem (as Bethlehem and Calvary are both set within many hills). Both Jesus' birth and death/Resurrection were foretold in advance (by prophecy), both were miraculous, and both involved God "emptying" Himself for us — each ultimately leading to our salvation.

Christ came to do for us what we could not do for ourselves. In both of these events, history and the future were irreversibly changed forever. How fitting that the two most important events in this drama we call history would be linked by the same cast of "characters." Bethlehem and Calvary were less than seven miles apart geographically; they are even closer in the heart of God.

MAKING IT PERSONAL

It may seem odd to consider the passion and death of Jesus on Calvary during the Advent and Christmas season, but looking at the parallels helps us to grow in appreciation not only for what God did for us, but how intentional He was from the beginning. This same God has a perfect plan for your life and His timing, likewise, is perfect. If you are struggling to see how God's plan is unfolding in your life right now, learn and pray this simple prayer, "Lord, I don't always understand you, but I trust you. Amen."

DAY TWENTY-FIVE

Over the past two dozen reflections, we have paused to consider what happened 2,000 years ago and to answer that original question from the Introduction, namely, "Why did God become man? Why did the Word become flesh?" And in case you're still wondering, you might be surprised to learn you already knew the answer all along. There is a line in the Nicene Creed that we pray at Mass: *"Begotten, not made, consubstantial with the Father; through Him, all things were made. For us men and for our salvation, He came down from heaven."* That's the short answer to the question. That's why God became man. God became man for our salvation. God is love, and *true love* works for the salvation of the other.

So, *what* are we supposed to learn from Christ in the New Testament that we couldn't or didn't learn about God before Christ's birth in the Old Testament? Well, put very simply, God became what we are to give us what He is; He came down to us so that we could get back up to Him.

Through the Incarnation, God meets us where we are — walking and pointing us to where we need to go. The Incarnation is simultaneously a simple truth and a profound mystery, a beautiful and joyful mystery.

Our Church unpacks this truth even further in the *Catechism* (456–463), offering us four distinct reasons why God emptied Himself and took on flesh in Christ Jesus.

1. He came to *reconcile* us with God.
2. He came that we might know God's *love*.
3. He came to model *holiness*.
4. He came so that we could become "partakers in the *divine nature*."

Now, there is a lot packed into all four of these ... that would necessitate another book, most likely. That fourth one, though, necessitates a second look. One of the reasons God became man is so that we could partake (take part in) His divine nature. God drew near and became man so that mankind could become like God, with His divine nature (Body, Blood, Soul, and Divinity) flowing through our veins every time we receive Holy Communion.

This is a deep mystery that the greatest saints have pondered and preached about for two millennia. There is no higher affirmation on the planet that God could give you than to dwell within you. Just as He was the greatest Christmas gift the world could fathom 2,000 years ago, He, Himself, is the greatest gift, still today. The key is to slow down long enough to appreciate what God is doing and all He has done. There is no darkness that can extinguish His Light. There is no sin greater than His mercy. God is still drawing near to us, each day.

Thank God for these seasons of Advent and Christmas! They are a constant reminder of His eternal presence with us.